D1156561

A Celebration Of
Hand-Hooked Rugs

A CELEBRATION OF

HAND-HOOKED RUGS

by
The Staff of *RUG HOOKING* Magazine

R·U·G
HOOKING
MAGAZINE
AND
STACKPOLE
BOOKS

Published by *RUG HOOKING* Magazine and
STACKPOLE BOOKS
Cameron and Kelker Streets
P.O. Box 1831
Harrisburg, PA 17105

Printed in Hong Kong

10 9 8 7 6 5 4 3 2 1

All photographs furnished by artist unless otherwise
credited.

Library of Congress Cataloging-in-Publication Data

**A Celebration of hand-hooked rugs/ the staff of Rug hooking
magazine.**
   p. cm.
   Includes index
   ISBN 0-8117-1867-0
   1. Rugs, Hooked. I. Rug hooking
NK9105.C45 1991
746.7'4'0922–dc20   91-4036
                                                      CIP
                                                      AC

CONTENTS

INTRODUCTION

Collecting the best examples of contemporary hand-hooked rugs is quite an undertaking. But since we publish the only specialty magazine devoted to this grand old folk art, we issued a call in RUG HOOKING Magazine—a contest for the best hand-hooked rugs—sat back, and waited. And the rug hookers across North America did not disappoint us. In came the entries, many more than we had hoped for. We held the judging in February and once we had seen the quality of the work, decided to put together a book of the winning rugs as a way of taking the show on tour.

Welcome to our Rug Hooking Show. In forty-eight pages of full-color shots, both full-lengths and close-ups, we've set up some outstanding examples of what is being created today with hook and wool. Spend all the time you want wandering among the rugs. We know you'll visit again and again, to enjoy these finely crafted works of art, to study them, to compare your own work with these blue-ribbon winners. The designs, colors, and variety of styles are inspiring.

But it isn't just the rugs we're showing off in these pages. We invite you to meet the artists as well. In the words of the hookers themselves, you'll discover helpful information. You'll learn how these stars got started, what encourages, motivates, and inspires them, how they find materials, teachers, and classes, how they help one another.

Just as among the rugs there is a mix of styles, there's no one profile of a model rug hooker. Some took up hooking after they'd retired from a career or raised a family and were looking for something to fill the empty hours. Some started young in fiber arts classes. Others wanted a hobby to do at home while they cared for young children. Some learned from neighbors, others from friends, and others from books.

On the chance that you haven't started your first hand-hooked creation and that you need a little encouragement, we hope this book helps. In seeing these magnificent rugs and reading the artists' stories, we hope you'll be encouraged to pick up the hook, take a strip of fabric in hand, and begin. To keep this folk art alive, growing, and healthy, we want to introduce hand-hooked rug making to as many friends as we can find. One day we'd like to see your work among these pages.

Winter's Eve

My inspiration for this piece was a Delft-type plate, and I asked Jane McGown Flynn to do the design. Jane warned me that a large, round rug would be hard to frame, but I was determined and when the pattern arrived, I was delighted–and challenged!

I went to my color planning swatches, knowing that I wanted the blues so prevalent in Delft, without any green overtones. I decided on two of Anne Ashworth's Green Mountain formulas: 16 and 18, which require only two dyes, blue and bright purple. Although these are eight-value swatches, I needed still lighter values, so I added additional, smaller spooning measurements to those in the formula. I finally came up with twelve-value swatches. I also added plain Dorr Natural 100% wool as the lightest color in each swatch. This gave me twenty-five values to work with. I dyed two of each swatch, and used 1½ times the amount of dye called for in the book. I used new wool and hooked into a burlap backing.

Even though I let my imagination run free when hooking the sky, I did follow the customary rules for hooking pictorials. Because the design is essentially monochromatic, I tried to place colors according to "distance" in the picture, using the middle values in the middle of the piece. The usually dark figures like trees, evergreens, and shadows are hooked with several values, and everywhere, I thought CONTRAST, which I feel is the key to the design. I did not try to use the swatches in any consecutive order, as is usually done with fine shading, but instead I pulled values at random. One thing I did learn: it is easy to use swatches efficiently. If I found I was using one value more frequently than another, I simply moved up or down, or to the second swatch.

I would like to be able to say that the clapboard effect on the little houses was a conscious, artistic, decision; it was not, but instead a fortuitous accident. I was running out of that particular value and decided to skip every other row and that's how I made the clapboards. I was also taught that an open door in a hooking signals a warm welcome to the viewer; but this is a cold New England night, so my doors stayed closed. To offset the inhospitable effect, I put lights in the house windows.

The church, with its pillared porch and darkened windows, was a challenge. By using medium-darks, I tried to give the building an air of strength and protectiveness, without making it brooding or Gothic.

The gazebo featured in the forefront of the picture was a delight to hook. I put colors and details everywhere and lots of very soft color, as well as white, in the foreground.

The sky is usually the last element hooked in a pictorial and mine was no exception. I used the many light and dark swatches I had left and no one was more delighted or surprised with the rather dramatic result than I.

"Winter's Eve" won first prize and best of show, Tioga County Fair Owego, New York; best small piece, Northern McGown Teachers' Workshop, Worcester, Massachusetts; and a blue ribbon for small pieces, McGown National Rug Exhibit, Chicago, Illinois, 1990.

I started rug hooking in 1976, under the instruction of Bernice Hunt. Upon her retirement in 1980 I began to teach both primitive and tapestry hooking. I regularly correspond with Claire DeRoos and attend Green Mountain and Western Pennsylvania rug schools.

"Winter's Eve" is 24 inches in diameter.

A Jane McGown Flynn pattern, number 1312, the rug is hooked with Dorr wool, cut on number three and hooked on burlap.

ELIZABETH BLACK

Elegant Floral

The rug was designed and hooked for Mr. and Mrs. John Townsend. The only stipulations given me were that it be a certain size, that it contain shades of red and brown, and that it be compatible with another larger rug that I had designed and hooked for the same room. The rug compliments the room's fine American antiques and picks up the colors of the landscape seen from the large windows which encircle the room.

If I hadn't left my eighteen-month-old daughter with her glass of water and paint brush to "paint" the window while I answered the phone, and if she hadn't discovered my oil paints and canvas were far more fascinating than water, I probably never would have searched for another hobby.

Shortly after the disaster with my oils, I saw an exhibit of hooked rugs at a local arts and crafts festival and thought hooking would allow me to continue to paint–with wool. The first instructor I approached refused

D. B. BROOKER

to teach me to hook because I wanted to design my own projects. Undaunted, I went to the local library, got a book, and taught myself.

My work consists mainly of commissioned pieces and occasionally a few pieces which are sold at juried

shows. Because I am totally self-taught my love of nature and animals has influenced my work. Custom work offers ongoing challenges in color and design.

And, now twenty-four years after I began hooking, I still find I am challenged and fascinated by what

can be created with wool strips and a hook. The years have been filled with juried shows, television and press coverage, designing kits and custom hooked pieces.

"Elegant Floral" is 4' x 6'4".

This rug is hooked on 100% cotton rug backing with new 100% wool fabric, which was cut in $3/32$ of-an-inch wide strips. Some of the colors were specially dyed and the remainder were standard colors purchased from woolen mills.

Wildwood

I planned this rug for my new enclosed sun room which overlooks the garden. I wanted the room to be an extension of a tranquil old New England garden and "Wildwood" is a walk through the New England woods in early spring.

The rug, as I planned it in Meredith LeBeau's class, presented two challenges. First, the flowers and plants were to be hooked botanically correct in color and form. I researched flora and dyed my swatches carefully.

The second and most difficult challenge was the leaves. I wanted a medium green background and therefore I chose no less than six green swatches for the leaves and plants. To avoid losing details or the graceful turnovers of the plants and flowers, I carefully placed each swatch. While the cut of the wool, hooked exclusively with number 5, follows the early primitive technique, the hooking and color planning adhere to the traditional tapestry methods of dyeing and workmanship.

"Wildwood" is 68" x 84".

The pattern was created by L.H. Zeiser.

CHRISTIE BRUNSON

Shangri-La: Weidner's Point

Though I have been interested in fiber arts all my life, I have only recently begun to hand-hook rugs. Having just moved to rural upstate New York, I visited Hanni Ivanoff, my new neighbor. She has hooked rugs for many years both as a remedy for her arthritis and as an economical way to cover her floors. I was impressed with her success on both counts and she has become my teacher and my inspiration.

Two things about hooking continue to amaze me: the textural surface created by looped fabric and the painterly potential of the medium. My designs are original, but not particularly primitive. Though all my rugs look quite different, they share a quality somewhere between the purely decorative and the purely representational. I have found that sometimes hooking a representational image in the primitive style will make the rug look decorative. I love the old hooked rugs and the best homage I can pay that tradition is to make pieces that honestly reflect my time and circumstances, as my mentors have done. I want to keep their lightheartedness and discover a contemporary way of joining form and function to equal theirs.

This piece is 51 inches in diameter.

"Shangri-La: Weidner's Point" grew out of my good fortune in relocating to the Catskill Mountains. The first in a series on the seasons, this rug depicts the winter view from my studio.

The rug was hand hooked with strips of polyester-knit fabric cut by hand. As was traditionally done, I used discarded clothing and chose whatever provided the most appropriate texture or color.

Curzon

I wanted to do a small Oriental rug to be used in the same room with a Persian rug. I chose "Curzon" and planned the colors to coordinate with the Persian. Dorr red #6-5 seemed the closest match to the main colors, and I used the Dorr red swatch for the red carnation-type flowers and the number six value of that swatch for the red stripes. Nancy Blood did the dyeing for the other colors. The blue for the main field is Green Mountain #16, value 8, and I used the swatch of that color for the blue flowers. The crown-shaped flowers were done with a swatch made with 1/32 Royal Blue, second CF spoon, over pink wool, the green leaves with Connie's Caldron 31, and the cream-colored center with 1/2 formula Stained Glass 13 over Dorr Natural. The strips were cut on the number-three cutter.

This rug was awarded a first-prize ribbon at the Tioga County Fair and a second prize at the National Exhibit in Chicago.

I have admired hooked rugs for as long as I can remember. The first rug class I can recall was held in a small town in northern Pennsylvania, Oakland, where I lived in the early fifties. I did not belong to the class because I had young children to care for and all the members were older ladies. When my three children were grown I began to pursue activities outside the home. I enrolled in a rug hooking class at a local museum/art center, Old Mill Village, in New Milford, Pennsylvania. Though I was unable to return to the class the following year I did continue to buy books and magazines about hand-hooked rugs and studied them from time to time, but I still lacked confidence to go ahead on my own.

In 1987 I moved to a Binghamton, New York to live with my

younger daughter, who shared my interest in hooked rugs. My daughter persuaded me to answer Nancy Blood's magazine ad and join her class. Nancy's enthusiasm for the art is contagious, and she is very generous with praise and encouragement. I now spend a lot of time hooking and often hate to leave it to take care of the necessary things in life, like eating, sleeping and cleaning!

"Curzon" is 24" x 36".

Pattern by Jane McGown Flynn.

The Wave

When a friend and I met to go hooking one day, we pooled our cars at Crescent Beach, a spot rather well-known on the South Shore of Nova Scotia. The day was particularly beautiful and we stopped a moment to watch thunderous waves crashing on the sandy beach. The waves were strong and full of Irish moss, being tossed in the air and pulled and pounded back into the sea, each wave as full as the last.

We must carry such images with us and not know we do so, but when a weaver gave me some thrums the very color of the Irish moss, I knew exactly what I wanted to do with them. I set about to create my wave. Another gift of fish leather, tanned nearby on Cape Sable Island, became the dark little fishes far out at sea.

An interesting note: The sea moss, used in Nova Scotia as a fertilizer, is spread directly on the land at spring planting time and plowed into the soil. After a storm this useful gift from the sea is gathered from the beach and loaded into tubs or plastic bags. You know it is a good day to go looking for sea moss when you notice droppings all along the road. I follow the trail back to the source much as Hansel and Gretel did with the crumbs of bread!

"The Wave" measures 27" x 55".

"The Wave" is hooked on a rug-warp backing with wool cut to #5 width and has a sleeve on the reverse side for hanging. It is not intended to be used on the floor.

ARLYN ENDE

Landing at Uraniborg

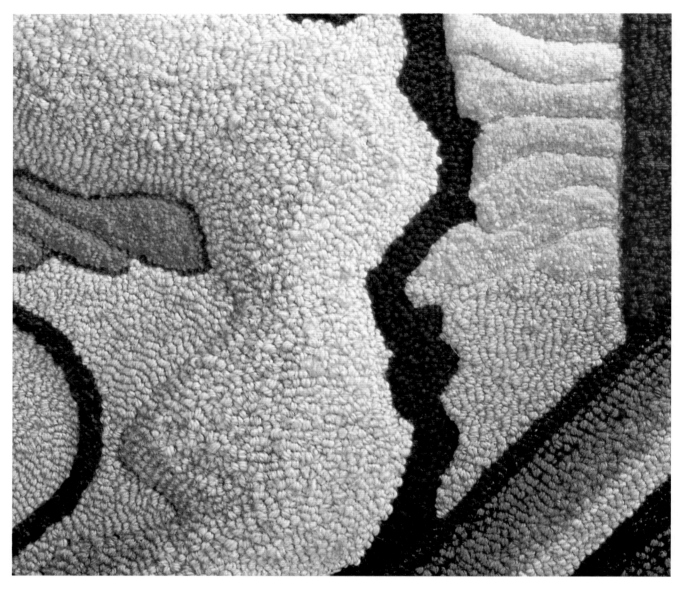

A CELEBRATION OF

In my work as a textile artist I enjoy creating objects that appeal to the eye and beg to be touched. Hooking is, for me, a seductive and spirited medium, and the floor is a challenging design surface for creating surprising effects and visual illusions.

To stretch the medium, and myself, in exciting new directions, I designed an L-shaped frameloom with a rolling warp that allows me to work from both sides of the textile. I find that the interplay of hooking and tufting techniques inspire, stimulate and focus the creative process.

I have maintained a textile studio at my farm in Bradyville, Tennessee since 1972. During the past twenty years I have received national recognition for my rugs and tapestries, which have been shown in major exhibitions and included in private and public collections throughout the United States. My room-sized rug "Tidal Pools" was awarded Grand Prize in the 1989 American Crafts Awards.

This piece measures 37" x 57".

"Landing At Uraniborg" was hooked on my A/E Frameloom with 100% wool yarns on a primary backing of 100% cotton foundation. Using the traditional hook, the punch needle and a hand rug tufter, I completed the rug in two months. The surface varies from one-fourth to one inch high and contrasts the looped texture with areas of carved and sculpted pile.

The rug was commissioned for the home of Richard A. Northcutt in Woodbury, Tennessee.

Winter Patterns

Looking out the window one winter day, I noticed different black and white patterns on the tree trunks and branches and in the stream and animal tracks on the snow. The snow-covered bushes were bowing ballerinas in white tutus. A cardinal pair flew by like a flash of fire. I put the scene into poetry, then transformed the poem into "Winter Patterns."

Wool-strip hooking is a medium in which your world is your pattern. I thought the drawn-on-backing pattern would be a good example to use to demonstrate tapestry techniques to my class, and it was ready just in time for the class I was teaching at the Region I ATHA workshop in Connecticut in 1989.

I began by hooking the big tree trunks, and the cardinals, then climbed the pines to reach their branches, set the branches against the sky and the distant woods, and then climbed back down through the hooking until I confronted the

squirrel tracks. The shadows on the snow were the hardest but most important part.

I finished this rug over the summer, framed and exhibited it in a month-long show sponsored by the Chelmsford Art Society and the

Massachusetts Council for the Arts in February, 1990. At the Eastern States Exposition it won a blue ribbon in the pictorial originals category.

"Winter Patterns" is 22" x 34".

Nantucket

Several years ago I saw a picture on a calendar, a snow scene. There was something about the balance of it, and I was drawn to it just by the name – Nantucket – one of my favorite places.

I always try to use symbolism in my pieces. I believe that symbolism is a bridge between the seen and the unseen worlds and while I hooked this rug I made many trips over that bridge.

First I hooked the church, to honor my unshakeable faith in God.

The clock shows the hour is four o'clock, approaching the end of the day and an evening of rest. I have just left the book shop and my youngest son, Ben, has run ahead with our dog to pick an apple from the tree. Our home is the blue house with the hooking room to the side.

"Nantucket" is 30 1/2" x 38".

Hooked with 100% wool.

Wildwood

Mrs. L.H. Zeiser's "Wildwood" captured my imagination as soon as I saw it pictured in the Heirloom catalogue, and no less than a 7' x 7' room-sized rug would do! Seven years later, off and on between many other projects, it is finished and on the floor. "Wildwood" is a quiet companion that knows me too well and does not disappoint. The pinks and rusts, purple violets and orange lilies are combinations that surprise and work.

Gardening is my first love. My childhood memories of growing up among the Amish farms of Lancaster, Pennsylvania, and working with Grandpa in his victory garden, are intertwined with those outrageous dahlias and first peas. It isn't surprising that I gain most pleasure in hooking flowers, fruits and vegetables.

Ask an addict how it began, and you might get the same mumbled replies and furtive evasions: two closets full of fabrics, bags of yarn in the attic, wardrobes of handmade clothes, and boxes of hand-knit sweaters replete with personalized labels. You are talking to a woman who cannot walk past a fabric store, who derives enormous pleasure from meandering up aisles just feeling fabrics – from Boston to Paris and from Cairo to Damascus.

ROBERT HANNUM

Fifteen years ago, Marilyn Lovell, my friend and fellow collector of bolts and skeins, said she'd just discovered a wondrous new world, full of wools and mills and, best of all, dye pots. She was "hooked" and soon so was I. My next step was to find a teacher. I must have done something right in a previous life to have found Meredith Lebeau. I arrived in her class with a 4' x 6' piece of burlap for an "Iris" rug. Meredith commented that most students begin more simply with a "Sue's Rose" cushion, but I naively said I preferred the irises. That then, she said, is how you shall begin. It is still my favorite rug and has won a blue ribbon in our local art association show. Hooking is now part of my life: my relaxation, my therapy, my way of satisfying the need to create something subtle, colorful and tactile.

"Wildwood" measures 7' x 7'.

An Heirloom pattern, #663A. Designed by L.H. Zeiser.

Gabriel

In "Gabriel" I explore the mystery of a mountain winter's night. The colors and forms are warm and reassuring, yet the shadow which "Gabriel" casts upon the land is flat, creating a surrealistic effect.

I shall never forget the first time I saw a hooked rug–at the Vermont Stratton Mountain Art Show. It was the artwork on the rug that caught my eye and drew me in, but it was the feel of the wool, its warmth and heft, that "hooked" me. I just had to learn how to make one of my own. Thirty or forty rugs later, I'm still hooking away.

This old-time medium has proved to be the perfect extension for my art and design background. Now my artwork is in a physical as well as intellectual relationship with the audience and, as an artist working in this venerable medium, I have the opportunity to express my twentieth-century view of the world and still be part of the fabric of our American past.

I am very strongly influenced by the beauty of the land here in Vermont, and I find that nature has a way of showing through in my work.

This rug is 42" x 28".

"Gabriel" is constructed of New Zealand and British fleeces which I have custom spun to my specifications. I then dye the yarn myself. The backing material is 100% cotton monk's cloth. The rug is hooked from the back in a continuous loop, using a craftsman's punch needle.

This rug was exhibited at the Northwinds Gallery in Woodstock, Vermont and is now in a private collection.

Grandma's Porch

This was my first experience working with a linen background. I found I had to adjust my style and hook much looser, because linen stretches so easily. I prefer the firmness of burlap because I can hook more closely.

The house pictured in the hand-hooked wall hanging is my husband's boyhood home near Staunton, Virginia. Parts of the house, including the part which is pictured, are over one hundred years old. The heavily stuccoed walls, thick beams and heavy framework, seem impermeable. Grandma and the family would sit in the old rocking chairs on the wrap-around porch, looking out over the rolling pasture land and the old spring house, cast in the shadows of the nearby weeping willow.

When our children were little, they spent many happy hours at Grandma Howell's, roaming the farm and rocking back and forth in the old porch swing. Grandma is gone now, our children are grown, and we don't see the old place much any more, but to preserve this nostalgic vignette for our children and our children's children, a hand-hooked wool rug seemed the perfect medium.

Hooking the stucco was fun. I used scraps of a rather heavy gray and cream houndstooth check, cut into strips, the lighter colors for the stucco and the darker ones for the shadows.

The biggest challenge was the large expanse of bare floor, the wide-planks quite in need of paint. I wanted the floor to add to the mood and not call attention to itself, so I delineated only a few planks at the top near the swing and began working my way down, attempting to achieve the planked effect with different textures and gradation of colors. I got about a third of the way down and was having difficulty seeing where the colors would take me, so I switched to the bottom and worked my way up. That was a challenge. I tried many combinations of fabrics and colors and dyed a lot of material to get the effects I wanted. Most of the fabric was shades of gray, overdyed with Rit's Country Blue.

I started hooking after I saw an announcement at a local recreation center. Having just retired from twenty-nine years of teaching, I was ready to get involved in creative and interesting activities. I had no idea what was involved in rug hooking, but after one session I was ready for more. Now Friday mornings are reserved for wool rug hooking with Roslyn Logsdon's class in Laurel, Maryland.

"Grandma's Porch" measures $16^1/2$" x $21^1/4$".

Egyptian Nights

"Egyptian Nights" began modestly enough. I was taking classes with Hallie Hall of Contoocook, New Hampshire and wanted to start a new project. In a book of early design motifs I had seen a swirling design with daisies in the big round circles. I was intrigued with the swirl–it looked to me like a comet–and I thought I might be able to adapt the design for a very contemporary rug for my bedroom.

Inspired by the colors of some sheets I had recently purchased, with Hallie's expert guidance, I put together the colors so the rug, when finished and on the floor, would look as if it could take off! The swirls were dip-dyed to achieve just the right highlights. The mauve background was the critical color to dye since it had to blend with both the sage green to dark blue and the apricot raspberry dip. I always like to incorporate some old favorite material from other rugs, and this time I used a bit of overdyed Woolrich plaid.

Even though this piece was hooked with material cut to $5/32$ of an inch, it took forever to hook

ANDREW EDGAR

around the swirls. Thank goodness Maryanne Lincoln taught me to hook in circles. Throughout the many classes at Hallie's, she and my fellow students wanted to know what I planned for the circles. I knew I did not want the daisies of the original Egyptian motif or three-fold symmetry, and I eventually settled on the triangle, which I think is just the right touch. I'm glad I didn't have the design worked out

until the last moment; it kept Hallie, my classmates, and me interested in the piece to the end.

"Egyptian Nights" won the Best-in-Show award at the League of New Hampshire Craftsmen's Living With Crafts exhibit at Sunapee, New Hampshire.

This piece is 30" x 38".

HAND-HOOKED RUGS

Raindrops on a Pond

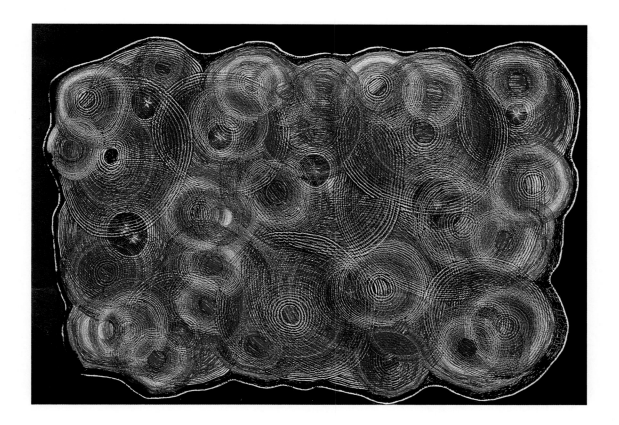

M y idea for "Raindrops on a Pond" developed, as most my hooking ideas do, slowly while I worked on another piece. An idea eventually emerged, but I confess that the idea was not truly complete until I was well into the hooking process.

I had read a book that suggested that there is geometry in everything around us, particularly in nature. I have found this to be true and I try to incorporate geometrical shapes into my hooked pieces because I see the shapes all around me. I am able to look at a tree, for instance, and identify the spirals, or concentric circles, that make up the trunk. In "Raindrops" I used triangles in the stars and placed them inside concentric circles.

My inspiration and ideas come most clearly as I take my daily walk through the woods near my home in Indiana. There I am able to see the interconnection between nature and man that inspired this piece.

I began hooking rugs while I was a student at Indiana University. I was taking a textile class and had to do a hooked piece as for a project. I've continued ever since.

"Raindrops on a Pond" is 57" x 81".

The Rooster

BRIAN McCRACKEN

BRIAN McCRACKEN

I began "The Rooster" rug in Jean Armstrong's primitive rug hooking class. I adapted the pattern from a greeting card, designed by Helen VanDenberg of Hayward, California, by tracing what I wanted of the design onto graph paper and then enlarging the design. Drawing larger squares on a sheet of plain tracing paper, I transferred the design square-by-square from the graph paper. Next I laid nylon tulle over the paper pattern and traced it with a black marking pen. I laid the tulle pattern over the monk's cloth backing and traced it yet again with a permanent marking pen to create a clear and lasting pattern.

I spot-dyed the reds and blues for the feathers and chose mottled wool for the body, using several different pieces of a color to get the right look and texture.

"The Rooster" rug now adorns a wall in my husband's study.

I began rug hooking about ten years ago after I fell in love with a hooked rug in a craft store. The $1500 price was out of my range, and since I've always been fairly good with my hands and I'm a patient worker I decided to try it myself. I saw no reason why I couldn't learn to do this sort of thing.

I found a teacher, Anne Ashworth, in Randolph, Vermont, and for ten years now I have attended her classes. She has been the greatest influence on my rug hooking. Her advice, "darken the shadow or lighten the highlight, or both!" works every time.

"The Rooster" measures 36" x 37".

This is a wall hanging, made of 100% wool, and hooked on monk's cloth. The wool is machine-cut in mostly $1/4$ or $3/16$-inch strips which were hand-dyed using dip-dyeing and spot-dyeing methods or casserole-dyed using over-dyeing, bleeding, and onion-skin-treating techniques. The rug is finished by cording and whip-stitching.

Story City

To celebrate the rich heritage of hand-hooked rug making, my entry had to be one that expresses a design indigenous to the Midwest, where I live. "Story City," a Prairie Craft House design of the Telemark style of rosemaling, is just that kind of pattern.

Since designs of this nature are Norwegian I felt I should use typical Nordic colors in the design. Carol Kassera of Prairie Craft House planned the colors.

The swatches were hand-dyed over white and natural Dorr wool, and the background is a commercial piece of Colonial Blue.

The first step in the actual process of hooking "Story City" was deciding where to place the colors in order to properly distribute the color plan. The scrolls were hooked with the darkest value toward the inside, and the lightest value outside. I hooked the background as I developed each scroll so I wouldn't lose the shape. I finished

the edges by whipping a crewel-type wool yarn, which had been dyed to match the background, and binding the raw edges of the burlap with tape.

My version of "Story City" won a second-place ribbon in the Rug Hooking Exhibit at Nordic Fest in Decorah, Iowa.

I started hooking in 1981 after seeing a demonstration given by a local teacher, Carol Kassera, and, with her encouragement, I entered a McGown training class. I continued

to take classes and earned my certification in 1984 from Ripley.

I have given many of my pieces to friends and relatives for Christmas, birthdays, and other special occasions. The rest hang on the walls of our home or adorn the floors.

$19^{1}/_{2}$" x $37^{1}/_{2}$".

A Prairie Craft House design, number D-1146.

CHRIS MERRYMAN

Prairie Trip Rug

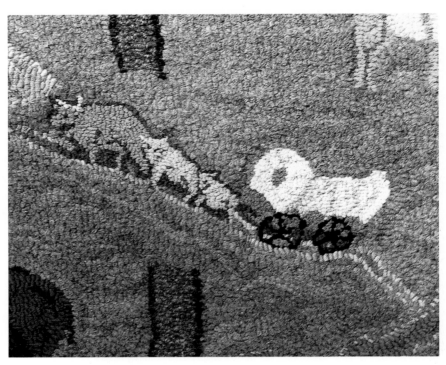

TOM MERRYMAN

In the best hooking tradition "Prairie Trip Rug" tells a personal story–of a family trip from Poulsba, Washington to Charleston, South Carolina, during which I visited my dear friend and first hooking teacher, Judy Gibbins. The rug is hooked mostly with as-is items given me by family and friends and with leftovers from other rugs. This piece was designed for use on the floor.

The background is an oat-colored fuzzy wool, scrunch-dyed with Cushing's Reseda Green to resemble prairie colors. I developed the design while I was in Charleston, and, at my request, Judy hooked her own house before I left, to commemorate our wonderful visit.

I incorporated elements into the design from postcards and photos of our trip, states' tourist pamphlets, free designs from *Rug Hooker, News and Views*, and magazine ads. Though the trip is over, the rug keeps vivid the memories of those thousands of antelope, the hardships of the Oregon Trail, and the grandeur of the mountains.

At the top of the rug are my home, dog, view, and points of local interest. At the bottom are Judy's home, pets, and area interests. In between are sights along the way: the Cascades, Bitterroots, Rockies, Bighorns and the Smokey Mountains; Custer's Last Stand; moose, antelope, coyotes, sheep, horses, cows, and buffalo; the Oregon trail

with wagon ruts in the rock, Register Cliff, Chimney Rock, and the North Platte River; farms; Bluegrass country, and, through it all, the winding road.

Rug hooking came into my life in 1986 in South Carolina when I met Judy Gibbins. Even though she was preparing to leave for vacation, she made time for one more hooker and

sold me an inexpensive frame, hook, burlap and a bag of scraps to practice with, and gave me a quick lesson to get me started. I couldn't see practicing without making something, so I sorted the colors, decided they suited a water scene, drew a crude pelican and started hooking. When Judy returned and saw my first creation, she knew I was hooked!

"Prairie Trip Rug" is 28" x 65".

Saugeen Range Light

My work is hooked as a tapestry; all the rows are horizontal. I believe it is unique to use the tapestry technique to hook a pictorial, and for me it was a challenge to make to colors bring out the curves. I dip-dyed and spot-dyed large pieces of fabric for the sky and the water of Lake Huron.

My rug depicts Chantry Island and the range lighthouse which guards the mouth of the Saugeen River. It is a very popular scene and has been called the most beautiful sunset in the world. For the design I used a photograph, taken by my son from our house, of the shore of Lake Huron and drew the outline of the dock and lighthouse on burlap. The wave action was formed as I worked the water.

The work has been framed in a mottled green to enhance the colors in the hooking.

My introduction to rug hooking came in 1980 when a friend invited me to Chatagua. I enrolled in the beginner's class under the guidance of Betty Swank. I returned from that week with many projects and lots of information. I was very impressed with Pearl McGown as she made her daily visits to the classrooms.

Since then I've attended several schools–from Sandy Lakes, Pennsylvania to the Ontario Hooking Craft School–and have benefited from the fine teaching of Margeurite Monthie, Bettie McClentic, Carol Garrity, Sally Newhall, Dorothy Haight and Marjorie Judson.

I am interested in original design and really enjoy planning and dyeing the wool so that when I hook all my rows horizontally, as in a woven tapestry, the colors come where I need them. In 1989 I won the design award at the Ontario Hooking Craft Annual Show. My large piece titled "Migration" pictured three Canada geese in flight. It, too, was hooked completely horizontally.

"Saugeen Range Light" is 22" x 30".

HAND-HOOKED RUGS

Cowscape

"Cowscape" is a typical Midwest scene of Holstein cows in pasture. While driving home from a nearby town, I pulled off the road to watch three cows standing close to the road. We spent a few minutes looking at each other until one cow (the one on the right) tired of me, turned, and walked away.

I didn't have a camera with me to photograph this scene, but the image remained and I returned a few days later to draw the scene. I sketched the landscape, but, because the cows kept their distance, I was forced to rely on imagination, memory and photographs I had taken previously.

To me these cows are special. In Wisconsin, as with the rest of the country, our small farms are disappearing and quickly being replaced by developments. These cows will live with me for a long time to come.

This piece measures 29^{1}/$_{2}$" x 38".

"Cowscape" is hooked on monk's cloth with wool fabric. It is an original design by Linda Petech.

Cabbage I

JOHN ROBERT WILLIAMS

My Puritan lap frame and Fraser cutter have been handed down to me from my husband's grandmother who was a student of Pearl McGown's. A thoroughly addicted hooker, I make about ten rugs a year. Most of my clients commission rugs depicting their homes, and these make up my cottage series. My clients are fascinating people and their homes are such interesting reflections of them, that it is a challenge to capture all of that in the rugs.

I live in an area surrounded by lakes; fish themes are very popular, and I have done a series of fish as well. I look forward to doing more designs of my own, rather than commissioned pieces. Because I am a painter, too, I plan to use some of my rug designs in floor cloths.

This is a 30" x 25" wool rug.

"Cabbage I" is an original design hooked with hand-dyed wool, of medium cut, on cotton warp backing.

to Dreams

CARL LEONARD STEWART

Carousels have figured prominently in my life. As a child, my grandmother Gregson took me to the pike in Long Beach, California to ride the merry-go-round. Years later, on my first date with my husband, I returned to that same merry-go-round.

"Into Dreams," which took three months to complete, began as many of my designs do–at the drafting table in my basement workshop. First drawn on artist's tissue, the pattern was transferred onto monk's cloth. I tried to see how small the piece could be and still be hooked in a manner which pleased me. The girl's face is only $1^1/2$ by $1^1/4$ inches, and the saddle and trappings on the pony are also very small and detailed.

I selected the colors and dyed the fabric, which I enjoy almost as much as the hooking. I used Dorr's white and natural wool, and hand dyed the fabric with formulas from "Anyone Can Dye for Making Rugs" by Clarisse Cox and "Shading with Swatches" by Clarisse McLain. I also referred to Joan Moshimer's "Jacobean Formulas" and "Imari Formulas."

I selected a sky-blue matte and a dark wood frame to complete the wall hanging. The design is set in a circle to carry out the theme of the brass ring and to suggest the continuous path of the carousel.

The hardest part to hook was the feather in the child's right hand. I wanted it to look light and fluffy, and I rehooked it so many times I

CARL LEONARD STEWART

thought the monk's cloth would fall apart!

"Into Dreams" is the first in a series of three original designs planned for "The Dream Series." Together they portray the happiness of a child in the night. In 1990, "Into Dreams" won a first-place blue in the wall hangings category at the Kansas State Fair, Hutchinson.

Out in the heartland of Kansas, it's not easy to find information about rug hooking. First you have to explain that you don't mean latch hook, then you must locate a teacher.

In 1981 I decided traditional, tapestry rug hooking was the folkart I wanted to learn, and the only

place I could think to go for help was the Topeka Public Library. I found "The Complete Rug Hooker" by Joan Moshimer and made my first piece–a chair seat hooked of old wool remnants.

My husband Carl who is as interested in rug hooking as I am, discovered in the back of the book the name of Margaret Hunt Masters, a teacher only eighty-five miles from our home! Mrs. Masters has been the major influence in my work. She has sharpened my eye for color and perfected my skill in fine tapestry hooking, particularly with facial details.

This piece measures $20^1/2$" across, and framed it is 27" square.

Fire Water

This rug celebrates the heritage of rug hooking because it is an example of how you can take an old simple rug design, in this case the agate pattern, and use it to create a rug that is a blend of new and old. Just as we are not exact copies of our ancestors, certain family characteristics tie us one to the other, and each succeeding generation is a fresh interpretation of the old.

I chose 6" squares for a structural effect that would be easy to hook but allowed myself creative freedom within each square to avoid exact repetition. I was able to use up an accumulation of odd beige wools, and I left all colors as-is, except the peach tones, which I dyed. I used size 6 and 8 cut strips and Scottish burlap foundation.

This was a fun rug to hook, because each square was a variation on the theme, and the variety kept my enthusiasm and interest throughout. I love the movement and color that evolved within the wavy lines, and the different connections each square has with the others. I now share a connection with that anonymous person who sat down one day and created the agate design, perhaps in a moment of whimsy, in what possibly was a very structured life.

"Fire Water" is 52" x 44".

Butch

As soon as I see an interesting picture or idea I know right away that I want to try it. It was just that way with "Butch." I saw the poster of an adorable little boy with his bag packed, ready to head out into the world by himself, and I knew it would make a wonderful rug.

I enjoyed hooking the tennis shoes the most. I was very careful to make sure that the laces were a little dirty in some places. It took me three hours to complete each sneaker, so I wanted them to have just the right touches.

The jacket was also interesting to construct. I used three different plaid wools for the jacket, and I used both spot-dyeing and swatches for the rest of the hooking. I've found that you just have to use what you have available.

In this area of Pennsylvania most people have never heard of traditional rug hooking. When my work is seen by people who are unfamiliar with rug hooking they are generally surprised that this type of art is being created. I love the look of the old-time hooked rugs, but I find new ideas in hooking very exciting.

I started hooking rugs in 1978. My sister was taking lessons at that time from Helen Talant in Michigan. I knew of no teacher in my area, so Helen sent me a preprinted pattern and wrote out instructions, and I tried to learn by mail. That didn't work. I went to Cedar Lakes Rug Camp for a week and Dotti Ebi was my teacher. She continued to teach me for a couple of years at Ripley in Michigan and gave me a good solid basis for hooking. She was always extremely generous with information and advice, and in time I was able to hook on my own. I continued to take classes from some of the best teachers in the country. I really think you need to do a lot of studying with good teachers before you try to develop techniques of your own.

"Butch" is 34" x 45".

The rug is hand-hooked with 100% wool.

BJV 1990

Tigris

For backing I used monk's cloth. I used 100% wool, which I dyed and cut into the finest strip. The basic colors are warm tawny, caramel in deep tones, mid and light values, and some white. To capture realism I hooked the dark stripes to move with the contours of the tiger's body. Just as finger prints are distinctive there are no two tigers with the same stripe pattern. I sketched the stripes loosely on the cotton backing and later defined them more carefully as I hooked them, sometimes using more, or deleting others.

By using many photographs for references I was able to draw the outline on the backing. I dyed the tawny color under the watchful eye of Maryanne Lincoln.

Elizabeth Black advised hooking the head first, the flanks and rear quarters next, and the middle part last. When it came time to do the arms, paws and feet, I was stumped. Almost all pictures of tigers show them in three feet of vegetation, so I never found helpful references. After studying the paws of stuffed toys and those of my own cat, I finally decided that the paws were going to be less defined, leaving the face and striped body as focal points.

I'm very fond of "Tigris." She's a family pet as well as a special charm, protecting my household and family from harm. We believe she brings us peace, serenity, and good fortune.

"Tigris" is 43" x 22$^{1}/2$".

HONORABLE MENTION

Janet Carija Brandt
Indianapolis, Indiana
Purple Cow

Louise Burt
East Dennis, Massachusetts
Chambwood

Elaine Carrier
Holliston, Massachusetts
Gabrielle's Garden/Pearl McGown's Lady's Delight

Sally Corbett
Bellevue, Washington
Flowers in Space

Carole Dale
Weirs Beach, New Hampshire
The Light of The Mind is Blue

Lois Dugal
Dover, New Hampshire
Father Christmas

Mary Evans
Atlanta, Georgia
Rosebud

Katherine Fisher
Mystic, Connecticut
Sunshine Flowers

Fay Fuller
O'oltewah, Tennesee
House Blessing/Liz Calloway design

Constance Grisard
Mitchellville, Maryland
Scottish Highlands

Jackye Hansen
Scarborough, Maine
Waldoboro Parrot/Jacqueline Designs

Norma Harper
Forest Lake, MN
Wild Beauties

Ruth Hood
Sunset Beach, North Carolina
The Messenger

Esther Jackson
Warwick, Rhode Island
Childhood Memories

Anne Jeter
Salem, Oregon
Snowy Egret/Jane McGown Flynn pattern

Kathleen Jones
Gaithersburg, Maryland
Fruit

Carol Kassera
Knoxville, Illinois
Persian Minature/Pearl McGown pattern

Joyce Krueger
Waukesha, Wisconsin
Geometric Quilt

Sarah Ladd
Long Island, Maine
Flora Portrayed

Fay Leischner
Hillsboro, New Hampshire
Hamadon/Pearl McGown pattern

Carol Lippincott
Philadelphia, Pennsylvania
Caribbean

Nancy Martineau
Seattle, Washington
Love Seat

Patricia Merikallia
New Canaan, Connecticut
Peaceable Kingdom

Janet Meyer
New Milford, Connecticut
Connecticut Stones

Linda Mickiewicz
Meriden, Connecticut
Old Deerfield Panel/Jane McGown Flynn pattern

Barbara Miller
Lakewood, Ohio
Chinese Rhapsody/Jane McGown Flynn pattern

Nancy Clark Miller
Sacremento, California
Agatha Antique/Pearl McGown pattern

Virginia Morong
Dexter, Maine
Doorstop Cat/Marion Ham pattern

Mary Murphy
Atlanta, Georgia
Empress/Pearl McGown pattern

Gladys Myers
Blachly, Oregon
Evans Brand

Betty Oberstar
Wilton, Connecticut
Hearts and Swans

Sarah Parker
Poland Spring, Maine
My Irish Cottage

Miles Parker
Poland Spring, Maine
Tabby

Suzanne Petretta
Pittsfield, Massachusetts
Wedding Rug/DiFranza Designs pattern

Jenna Price
Frederictown, Ohio
Story on Stairs

Jean Rowland
Pittsburgh, Pennsylvania
Crazy Cats

Ura Scott
Decatur, Tennessee
Little Rest/Heirloom Design

Jule Marie Smith
Ballston Spa, New York
Vermont Farm

Joan Stocker
Reading, Massachusetts
My Church

Kristine Sullivan
Newtown, Connecticut
Matisse Goldfish, a Reflection

Arlyne Taddeo
Chagrin Falls, Ohio
Desert Shield

Patricia Tritt
Atlanta, Georgia
Patrick's World

Lois Trout
McCordsville, Indiana
Fruit Basket Medley

Marcy Van Roosen
Ashland, Massachusetts
October Wedding Rug

Elsie Van Savage
Brunswick, Maine
Fred and Ginger

Jane Westlake
Cobourg, Ontario
Porcelain Vase/J.R. Ogilvie design

Jan Whitaker
Holyoke, Massachusetts
Kandinsky's Yellow Point

Suzie Wilson
Barre, Vermont
Great Blue

Margaret Wolf
Sun City, Arizona
Teec/Jane McGown Flynn pattern

Mary Paul Wright
Atlanta, Georgia
Tennessee Contentment

SUPPLIERS

APPLETON KRAFTS & SUPPLIES
50 Appleton Ave
S.Hamilton, MA 01982
Complete line of rug hooking supplies.

CARIJARTS
2136 Silver Ln. Dr.
Indianapolis, IN 46203
Unique patterns for rug hooking.

GLORIA CROUSE
4325 John Luhr Road, N.E.
Olympia, WA 98506
Contemporary hooking supplies, books, videos.

DKS DESIGNS
P.O. Box 202
Mt. Calvary, WI 53057-0202
Complete line Traditional and Primitive hooking patterns. Featuring the Austrailian Collection. Catalog available.

DESIGNS TO DREAM ON
Jane McGown Flynn, Inc.
P.O. Box 1301
Sterling, MA 01564
Complete line of supplies for traditional and tapestry rug hooking. Catalog available.

DIFRANZA DESIGNS
25 Bow St.
North Reading, MA 01864
Patterns and kits for rugs. Complete line of rug hooking supplies. Catalog available.

DORR FABRICS
P.O. Box 88
Guild, NH 03754
Wool fabric, pre-cut Potpourri stripettes, rug hooking kits.

DOTTI EBI
501 Kingsbury
Dearborn, MI 48127
Dyeing information, supplies, and books.

EMMA LOU'S HOOKED RUGS
8643 Hiawatha Rd.
Kansas City, MO 64114
Primitive rug patterns printed on monk's cloth or burlap.

FORESTHEART STUDIO
21 South Carroll St.
Frederick, MD 21701
Rug Hooking, weaving, spinning, and other uncommon fiber arts. Supplies, equipment, instruction, and finished work.

GINNY'S GEMS
5167 Robinhood Drive
Willoughby, OH 44094
American Indian and Oriental patterns. Acid dyes and formula booklet. Catalog available.

HEIRLOOM CARE, INC.
P.O. Box 2540
Westwood, MA 02090
Rug cleaner for the professional care of hooked rugs. Includes natural fiber brush and complete instructions.

LANCASTER COUNTY FOLK ART
Pat Hornafius
113 Meadowbrook Lane
Elizabethtown, PA 17022
Primitive hooked rugs, supplies, commissioned work, videos.

MAYFLOWER TEXTILE COMPANY
P.O. Box 329
Franklin, MA 02038
Manufacturers of the Puritan Lap Frame.

MORTON HOUSE PRIMITIVES
9860 Crestwood Terrace
Eden Prairie, MN 55347
Complete line of supplies for primitive rugs. Catalog available.

NEW EARTH DESIGNS
Beaver Rd., RR 2, Bx. 301
LaGrangeville, NY 12540
Patterns silk screen printed on burlap, rug warp, monk's cloth and 100% linen. Catalog available.

JANE OLSON
P.O.Box 351
Hawthorne, CA 90250
Complete line of supplies for rug hooking and braiding. Catalog available.

PRO CHEMICAL & DYE, INC.
P.O. Box 14
Somerset, MA 02726
Commercial dyes, pigments, and auxiliaries for the surface coloration of fiber. Catalog available.

RIGBY CUTTERS
J.D. Paulsen
P.O. Box 158
Bridgton, ME 04009
Hand-maneuvered cutting machine that creates strips for hooking.

RUG HOOKING **Magazine**
Cameron & Kelker Sts.
P.O. Box 15760
Harrisburg, PA 17105
Today's finest source of information on traditional hand-hooked rugs. Provides how-to's, historical profiles, dye formulas, patterns and much more – in spectacular color.

RUG HOOKER STUDIO
P.O. Box 351, North Street
Kennebunkport, ME 04046
Complete line of supplies for rug hooking.

RUTH ANN'S WOOL
R.D. #4, Box 340
Muncy, PA 17756
100% wool, Natural, White and 28 colors, for rug hooking.

SEA HOLLY HOOKED RUGS
at Sea Holly Square
1906 N. Bayview Dr.
Kill Devil Hills, NC 27948
Wool, hand-dyed, by the yard, or pound. Finished pieces and rug hooking supplies also available.

SWEET BRIAR STUDIO
866 Main St.
Hope Valley, RI 02832
Patterns and supplies for Traditional and Primitive rugs. Catalog available.

THE TRIPLE OVER DYE FAMILY
187 Jane Dr.
Syracuse, NY 13219
How-to booklets with formulas for Triple Over Dyeing.

THE WEAVER'S LOFT
Roslyn Logsdon
Montpelier Cultural Arts Center
12826 Laurel-Bowie Road
Laurel, MD 20708
Teacher, supplier, commissioned work.

YANKEE PEDDLER
57 Saxonwood Road
Fairfield, CT 06430
Supplier of wool fabric, kits, dyed fabric and advice.

BALLOT

Welcome to this Celebration of Hand-Hooked Rugs. We would like very much for you to help us decide on the best of the best of these spectacular works of art. We invite you to cast a ballot for your favorite hand-hooked rug.

Mark your ballot well, and thoughtfully, please. Send it to us at your earliest convenience; reasonable facsimiles gratefully accepted (postmarked by January 1, 1992).

Then, show these pages and all that follow to your family, friends and neighbors.

Take your time, browse through the pages, explore each rug and get to know the maker. Let us know what you think. It won't be an easy choice to make...

Winners will be announced in the issue of *RUG HOOKING* Magazine directly following the processing of all ballots.

READER'S BALLOT
FOR BEST OF SHOWCASE
OF A CELEBRATION OF HAND-HOOKED RUGS

Please indicate the title of the rug, last name of the maker, and the page number.

1.) 1st Choice: _____

2.) 2nd Choice: _____

3.) 3rd Choice: _____

Additional comments: _____

_____

_____

_____
your name and address

_____
city/state/zip code

Send your ballot to:
Rug Hooking Magazine
P.O. Box 15760
Harrisburg, Pennsylvania 17105

INDEX